First World War
and Army of Occupation
War Diary
France, Belgium and Germany

63 (ROYAL NAVAL) DIVISION
Royal Marine Brigade
Headquarters
26 August 1918 - 12 October 1918

WO95/3108/1

The Naval & Military Press Ltd
www.nmarchive.com
Published in association with The National Archives

Published by

The Naval & Military Press Ltd

Unit 10 Ridgewood Industrial Park,

Uckfield, East Sussex,

TN22 5QE England

Tel: +44 (0) 1825 749494

www.naval-military-press.com

www.nmarchive.com

This diary has been reprinted in facsimile from the original. Any imperfections are inevitably reproduced and the quality may fall short of modern type and cartographic standards.

© **Crown Copyright**
Images reproduced by permission of The National Archives, London, England, 2015.

Contents

Document type	Place/Title	Date From	Date To
Heading	WO95/3108-1		
Miscellaneous	Royal Marine Brigade		
Miscellaneous	Overseas Operations. R.M. Brigade 1914. Action.	26/08/1918	12/10/1918

W095/3108(1)

W095/3108(1)

Army Form C. 2118.

ROYAL MARINE BDE
1st AUG — 1914

WAR DIARY
or
INTELLIGENCE SUMMARY.
(Erase heading not required.)

		Summary of Events and Information	Remarks and references to Appendices
			REMARKS.
		OVERSEAS OPERATIONS. R.M. BRIGADE 1914.	
		ACTION	
	on.	Embarked at SHEERNESS in H.M. Ships for passage to OSTEND.	
28th – 30th Aug.	"	Disembarked at OSTEND, starting 0500 and occupied Outpost Line covering Southern and Eastern approaches to Town.	No contact with the enemy
31st Aug.	"	In occupation of the above line.	
1st Sept	"	Re-embarked in H.M. Ships during afternoon and sailed for SHEERNESS. Arrived SHEERNESS 1030.	
19th Sept	Brigade H.Q. Chatham Battalion Portsmouth " Plymouth " Deal "	Embarked at DOVER in the forenoon and sailed in Transports for DUNKIRK, arriving late in the afternoon and marched into billets.	
19th – 23rd Sept.	(DUNKIRK) " " " "	Training at DUNKIRK. During afternoon 21st inst Brigade was fitted with khaki clothing on the Quays in DUNKIRK Harbour. Caps, puttees and chevrons deficient.	
24th Sept.	"	Brigade moved into Camp on CHAMP de MANOEUVRES.	
25th – 27th.	"	Training.	

Army Form C. 2118.

WAR DIARY
or
INTELLIGENCE SUMMARY.
(Erase heading not required.)

Royal Marine Bde — 1914 Oct

Instructions regarding War Diaries and Intelligence Summaries are contained in F. S. Regs. Part II. and the Staff Manual respectively. Title pages will be prepared in manuscript.

Place	Date	Hour	Summary of Events and Information	Remarks and references to Appendices
			OVERSEAS OPERATIONS. R.M. BRIGADE 1914.	REMARKS.
			ACTION	
	26th Aug.		Embarked at SHEERNESS in H.M. Ships for passage to OSTEND.	
UNIT. Brigade H.Q. R.M.A. Battalion. Chatham " Portsmouth " Plymouth "				
(O S T E N D)	27th Aug.		Disembarked at OSTEND, starting 0500 and occupied Outpost line covering Southern and Eastern approaches to Town.	
"	28th – 30th Aug.		In occupation of the above line.	} No contact with the enemy
"	31st Aug.		Re-embarked in H.M.Ships during afternoon and sailed for SHEERNESS.	
"	1st Sept		Arrived SHEERNESS 1030.	
Brigade H.Q. Chatham Battalion Portsmouth " Plymouth " Deal	19th Sept		Embarked at DOVER in the forenoon and sailed in Transports for DUNKIRK, arriving late in the afternoon and marched into billets.	
(D U N K I R K)	19th – 23rd Sept.		Training at DUNKIRK. During afternoon 21st inst Brigade was fitted with khaki clothing on the Quays in DUNKIRK Harbour. Caps, puttles and chevrons deficient.	
"	24th Sept.		Brigade moved into Camp on CHAMP de MANOEUVRES.	
"	24th–27th.		Training.	

Army Form C. 2118.

WAR DIARY
or
INTELLIGENCE SUMMARY.
(Erase heading not required.)

Instructions regarding War Diaries and Intelligence Summaries are contained in F. S. Regs., Part II. and the Staff Manual respectively. Title pages will be prepared in manuscript.

Place	Date	Hour	Summary of Events and Information	Remarks and references to Appendices
Brigade H.Q. Chatham Battalion " Plymouth " Deal " (C A S S E L)	28th Sept. 3rd Oct.		Moved to CASSEL and carried out operations in Motor-buses in conjunction with Armoured Cars in HAZEBROUCK Area.	Details of Armoured Car operations under Commander Samson R.N. are unknown. A large portion of the personnel was R.M., Major Armstrong, Risk, Capt Lathbury Capt.Coode & Lt Williams R.M.A are believed to have been in this unit.
Portsmouth Battalion (L I L L E)	28th Sept.		Moved to LILLE and occupied approaches on South, East and North of the Town with Machine Guns mounted in Lorries. On 1st Oct. Portsmouth Bn (less 1 Co) moved by rail to BAISIEUX and covered withdrawal of French Territorials from TOURNAI to LILLE. On the afternoon of the 2nd Oct. contact with German Cavalry Patrols was made by Lorry Outposts covering Town.	
Brigade H.Q. Chatham Battalion " Portsmouth " Plymouth " Deal " (A N T W E R P)	3rd Oct.		Moved by Rail to ANTWERP detraining at VIEUX DIEUX about midnight into billets.	
" " " " "	4th Oct.		Marched to LIERRE, arriving about 1100, and took over line from Belgian troops, as follows:- Chatham Battn. on right, Plymouth Bat tn. in the centre and Deal Battn. on the left from a point on the CONTICH-LIERRE railway 2,000 yards due West of LIERRE to the River NETHE at LISP. Portsmouth Bn. in Reserve on LIERRE-BOUCHOUT Road, 500 yards in rear of centre of the line. Hostile artillery active.	WAR NOMENCLATURE REPORT. Defence of ANTWERP 4th-10thOct.
" " " " "	5th Oct.		Advanced Posts on River NETHE driven in. Portsmouth Bn. occupied Belgian trenches on right of Chatham Bn. which had been evacuated by the Belgians, but was relieved again by Belgian troops at nightfall. Hostile artillery, machine gun and rifle fire active during day, on trenches and approaches.	

Army Form C. 2118.

WAR DIARY
or
INTELLIGENCE SUMMARY.
(Erase heading not required.)

Instructions regarding War Diaries and Intelligence Summaries are contained in F. S. Regs., Part II. and the Staff Manual respectively. Title pages will be prepared in manuscript.

Place	Date	Hour	Summary of Events and Information	Remarks and references to Appendices
	6th Oct.		Brigade retired to an intermediate position, Wood West of DONK-HOE DUIYK, which was occupied about 1230.	
	7th Oct.		Retirement from the above intermediate position Commenced about 0300, and Brigade marched inside inner ring of forts, and was placed in Div.Reserve in the neighbourhood of WAESDONCK.	
Chatham Battalion.	8th Oct.		Sent from Reserve to re-inforce Belgian troops in vicinity of Fort No.7 marching off about 1000.	
Portsmouth Battn.			Sent from Reserve to re-inforce Hendersons Naval Brigade in vicinity of Fort No.2 marching off about 1630 and coming under Commodore Henderson's orders on arrival.	
Plymouth Battalion Deal	" " " " " "		Ordered to retire from ANTWERP to ST. NICHOLAS by Colonel Seely and moved off about 1900. Brigade H.Q. remained in ignorance of these instructions, but on ascertaining that Battalions had retired, themselves left about 2150. The retirement of the Brigade was thus affected by units independently. The Chatham Bn. it is believed also moved under orders of Col. SEELY, whilst Portsmouth Bn. formed the Rearguard to Henderson's Naval Brigade.	Colonel Seely was not "part of" Maj.Gen.Paris's Command vide Maj.Gen Paris's despatch to the SECRETARY of the ADMIRALTY dated 31.10.14.
Brigade H.Q. Chatham Battalion Plymouth " Deal "	9th Oct.		Marched throughout the night and after being diverted from ST. NICHOLAS reached ST. GILLES-WAES about 0900. Entrainment in refugee trains for OSTEND was completed at about 1100.	
Portsmouth Bn. " "			Portsmouth Bn. together with Henderson's Naval Brigade was reported missing, but the Portsmouth Bn. actually did entrain at ST.GILLES-WAES late in the afternoon. By that time the Germans had cut the railway at MOREEKE, and the Bn. had to fight its way out in the darkness. In this action about 2 Companies under the Reg.Sergeant Major were captured. The remainder, however, marched to SELZAETE and again entrained, reaching OSTEND on the morning of the 10th Oct.	

Army Form C. 2118.

WAR DIARY
or
INTELLIGENCE SUMMARY.
(Erase heading not required.)

Instructions regarding War Diaries and Intelligence Summaries are contained in F.S. Regs., Part II and the Staff Manual respectively. Title pages will be prepared in manuscript.

Place	Date	Hour	Summary of Events and Information	Remarks and references to Appendices
Brigade H.Q. Chatham Bn. Portsmouth Bn. Plymouth Bn. Deal Bn.	10th Oct.		Embarked in Transport HONORIUS for ENGLAND.	
(O S T E N D)	11th Oct.		Transport sailed in late afternoon and hove to in OSTEND "roads" for the night.	
"	12th Oct.		Brigade arrived at DOVER in afternoon and proceeded by rail to Depot, R.M. DEAL.	Casualties during ANTWERP Operations. R.M.Brigade. Killed 23 Wounded 103 Missing 388. Authority Maj.Gen Paris's Despatch dated 31.10.14.

www.ingramcontent.com/pod-product-compliance
Lightning Source LLC
Chambersburg PA
CBHW081517160426
43193CB00014B/2719